INSPIRED INNER GENIUS

Anne Frank

In 1947, Anne Frank's Diary of a Young Girl was made into a book so the world could know her brave story. Anne was a Jewish girl who lived during World War II. Though the last few years of her life were spent in fear, hiding from the Nazis[1], Anne shows us her courage, love for learning, and belief in people through the words in her diary.

Anne was born in Germany in 1929. Before she was three years old, Anne, her parents, and her older sister Margot moved to a different country called the Netherlands. Germany had become a dangerous place for the Frank family to live.

At this time, German leaders, called Nazis, blamed the country's problems on Jewish people. Jews[2] had to wear yellow badges with a star so people could recognize them. Since the Franks were Jewish, they decided to escape the fear and hatred growing in Germany.

Anne was happy growing up in Amsterdam where she learned the Dutch language. She loved school and her friends. For her 13th birthday, Anne's parents let her choose a diary[3] as a gift. She chose one with a red and white checkered pattern.

Unfortunately, World War II was spreading across Europe. The German army took over many countries, including the Netherlands. Many Jews were captured, but some found ways to hide. The Frank family went into hiding on July 6, 1942, just a couple of weeks after Anne's 13th birthday.

Anne's family hid in an annex, a small apartment, behind her father's business. They shared this space with one of her father's employees and his family, and an acquaintance[4] who was a dentist. Because they were Jewish, these eight people had to stay quietly inside, every day, so they weren't found and captured.

Thankfully, there were many good people who wanted to help the Jews. Some of Mr. Frank's employees helped the annex group get supplies even though it was dangerous. Anne especially loved Miep's visits. Miep and others risked their lives to help families like the Franks.

It was hard to hide in the small annex with 7 other people. Anne shared her thoughts and feelings in her diary, like it was a friend. She even named her imaginary friend Kitty! Anne wrote to Kitty daily and grew to love writing.

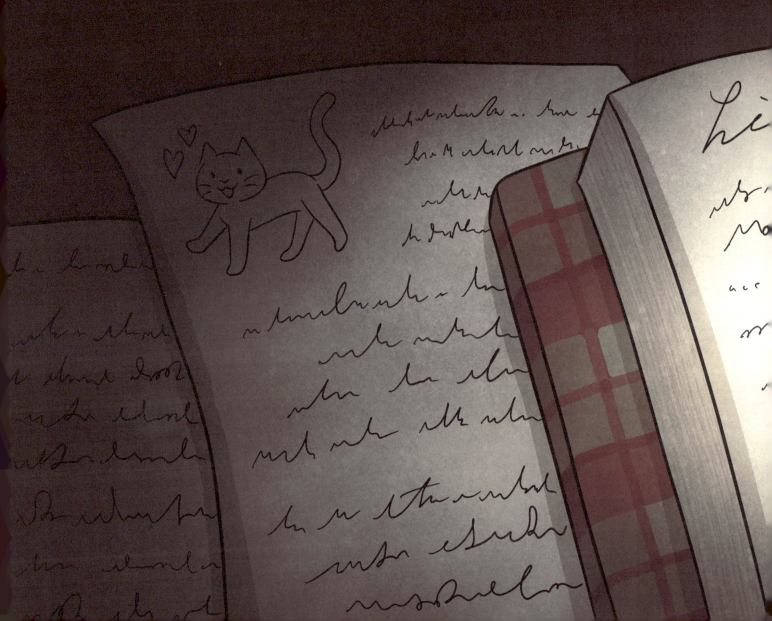

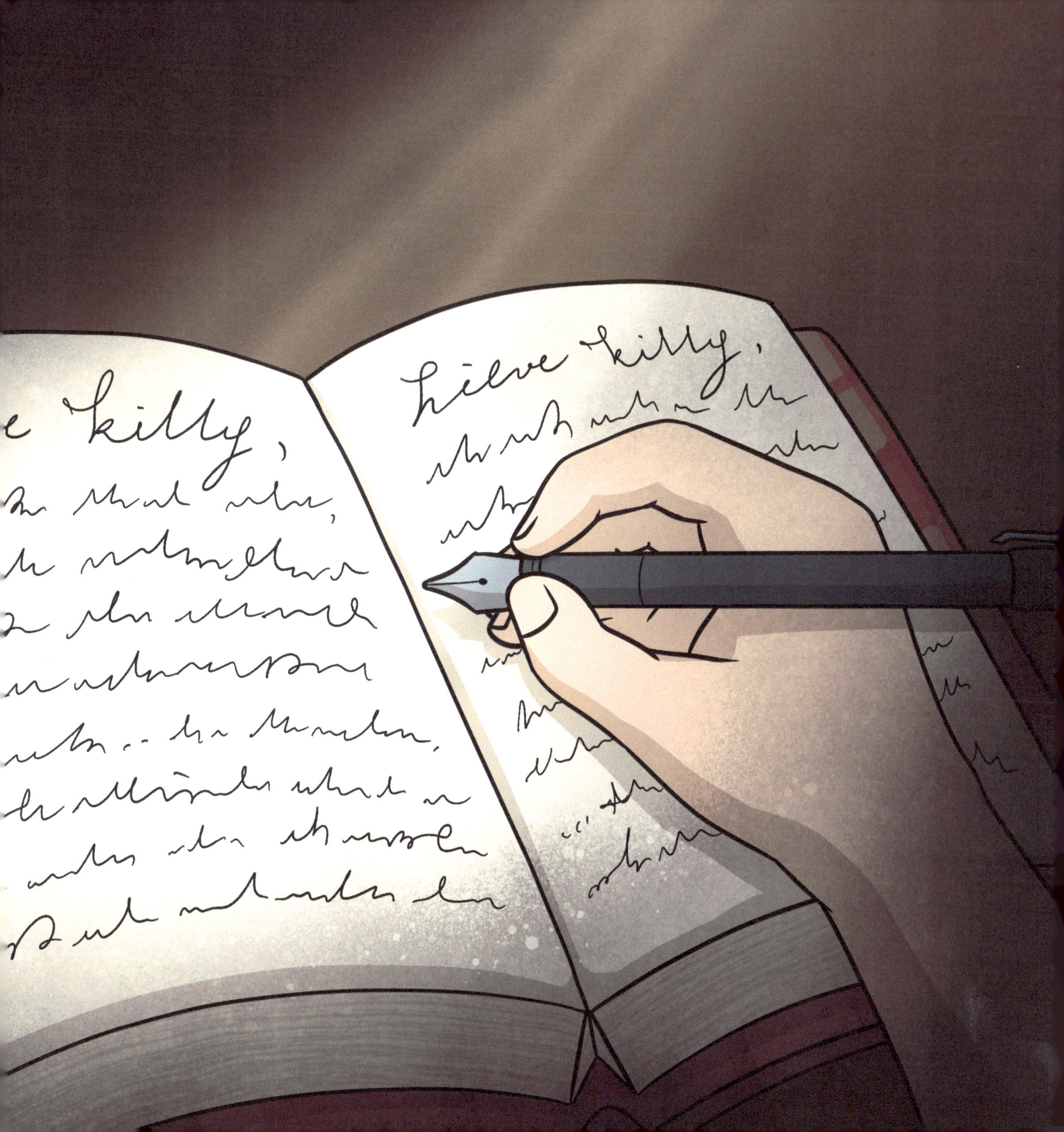
kitty,
Lieve kitty,

Though Anne's family and the others couldn't leave the annex, there were chores for keeping busy and a radio when it was safe. Anne loved to read biographies and history. She studied languages, math, and science. Anne started to dream that her diary would become a book called The Secret Annex.

Every day, the annex group stayed brave and hoped for peace, safety, and freedom. Sadly, the Nazis raided hiding places to find Jewish people and punish them along with their helpers. Anne's annex group was found on August 4, 1944, after 761 days in hiding.

Anne and her family were taken back to Germany at Bergen-Belsen. This place was one of the concentration camps[5] set up by Nazis to get rid of Jewish people. Anne and her sister got a disease called typhus[6], and they died in this camp in February of 1945. Anne was only 15 years old.

Anne's father Otto survived the concentration camp. He returned to the Netherlands and found that Miep had saved Anne's diary! Otto understood his daughter's dream of publishing a book. In 1947, Anne Frank's diary was published so the world could read her story.

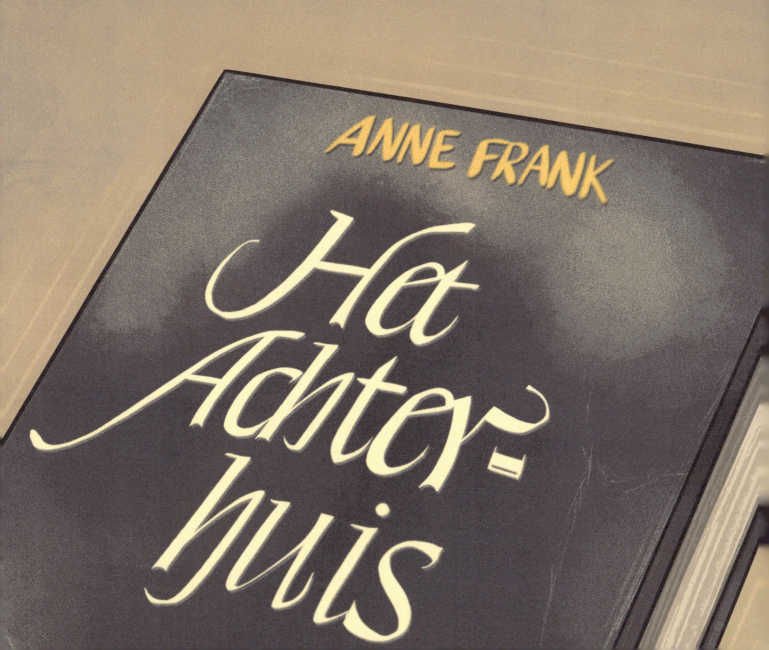

ANNE FRANK

Het Achter-huis

Though Anne Frank only lived to be 15, her bravery is inspiring. By writing her story, she showed the world how persecution[7], war, fear, and hatred affected her Jewish family. Anne's story gives us hope in courageous people who fight injustice[8] and strength in love and family. Her most powerful words are: In spite of everything I still believe that people are really good at heart.

GLOSSARY

1. Nazis — Group of people led by Adolf Hitler that came to power in Germany in the 1930s that persecuted Jews and other people.

2. Jews — Someone who practices Judaism as a religion or identifies as Jewish.

3. Diary — A book with blank pages inside that usually comes with a lock and key for writing private thoughts.

4. Acquiantance — A person one knows slightly, but who is not a close friend.

5. concentration camp

A harsh place where people are taken and held prisoner just because of what they believe or who they are.

6. Typhus

A contagious bacterial disease that causes a very high fever, terrible headache, and dark red rash.

7. Persecution

Hostility and ill-treatment towards someone considered different.

8. Injustice

Lack of fairness or justice.

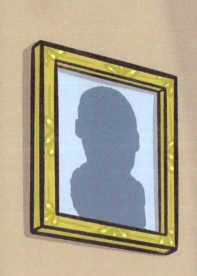

Muse Museum

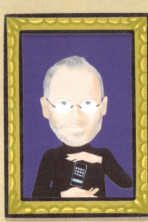

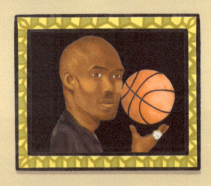

More **IIG** muses
to come...

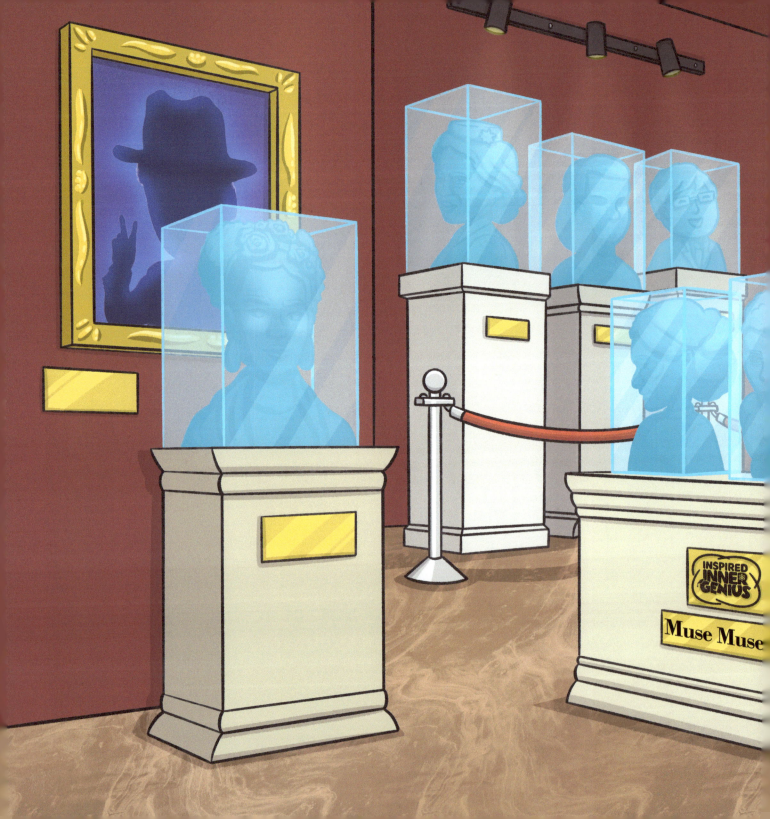

More 🎓 IIG muses to come

Anne Frank

1929 - 1945

Anne Frank was born in Germany in 1929. As Adolf Hitler and his Nazi party rose to power, German Jews were persecuted. The Frank family fled to the Netherlands where they lived for nearly a decade before World War II spread across Europe. With the Nazi invasion, the Frank family went into hiding in a "secret annex" in 1942. Just over two years later, Anne's family and the others in the annex were discovered.

Taken to an extermination camp in Auschwitz, Anne, her sister Margot, and her mother worked in the labor camp. Later, Margot and Anne were sent to Bergen-Belsen where they died of typhus. Anne was just 15 years old.

Anne Frank's father survived and returned to the Netherlands after the war. He found that Anne's diary had been saved and it was published in June 1947. Since then, Anne's diary has been published in over 70 languages so future generations can learn her story.

In 1960, the Anne Frank House in Amsterdam became a museum. Visitors can tour the rooms and see personal items, including Anne's original red-checked diary. Anne Frank was a brave young woman and talented writer whose story is a history lesson for all.

Dit is een foto, zoals
ik me zou wensen,
altijd zo te zijn.
Dan had ik nog wel
een kans om naar
Holywood te komen.
Anne Frank.
10 Oct. 1942

(translation)
"This is a photo as I would wish
myself to look all the time. Then
I would maybe have a chance to
come to Hollywood."
Anne Frank, 10 Oct. 1942

Anne Frank, German Jew who emigrated with her family to the Netherlands during the Nazi period. Separated from the rest of her family, she and her sister died of typhoid fever in the concentration camp Bergen-Belsen.

Here at Inspired Inner Genius, we believe that every child is born a genius. Join us in our journey to inspire the world, one child at a time.

Photographic acknowledgement (page 35) Anne Frank, German Jew who emigrated with her family to the Netherlands during the Nazi period. eparated from the rest of her family, she and her sister died of typhoid fever in the concentration camp Bergen-Belsen.
© ullstein bild via Getty Images

Cover designed by Irina Katsimon · Interior designed by Aimee Hawk ·
Published by Inspired Inner Genius

GRAB YOUR FREE EDUCATIONAL GUIDE!

This curated guide is the perfect educational tool to center a class around, to bring up at the dinner table, or even to spark an enriching conversation just before bedtime. Scan the QR code or visit us at **go.inspiredinnergenius.com/eg** to obtain yours!

Lightning Source UK Ltd.
Milton Keynes UK
UKHW051440190122
397371UK00002B/100